The Destiny Blueprint:
Unlocking Success through Discipline

JOHN M. LOPEZ

INTRODUCTION

Throughout history, humanity has been captivated by the notion that there might be a grand design or higher purpose governing the course of our lives—an invisible thread that weaves together the events, choices, and circumstances that shape our destinies. This age-old concept, often referred to as "The Destiny Blueprint," has been a subject of contemplation, wonder, and debate across cultures and belief systems.

A destiny blueprint implies that each person's life follows a predefined route, as though led by an elaborately crafted plan. It evokes ideas of fate, destiny, karma, and divine intervention, connecting human experience with ideas of greater forces at work. For some, this belief provides consolation in times of uncertainty, giving them a sense of purpose and significance in the face of life's ups and downs. Others may be piqued with curiosity and a desire to comprehend the interconnection of all things and our place in the great fabric of existence.

For ages, philosophers, spiritual leaders, and scientists have debated whether existence follows a predetermined course or if free will allows us to design our own destinies. Skeptics contend that the concept of a destiny blueprint might lead to passivity, in which people feel tied by a predetermined fate, restricting their capacity to take control of their life. Proponents of the notion, on the other hand, take solace in the belief that every event, whether joyful or difficult, has a purpose and adds to human progress.

We go on a quest to solve the riddles of life, meaning, and the interconnection of the human experience as we dig into the enigma of the destiny blueprint. We want to obtain insights about our existence, the role of choices and circumstances, and how belief in destiny or the power of choice shapes our perspective of life's significance via this inquiry.

In this discourse, we'll contemplate the significance of synchronicity and the intricate web of cause and effect that connects us all. We'll ponder the age-old question of whether destiny is an immutable force, gently guiding us along the path, or a malleable concept shaped by our thoughts, actions, and beliefs.

The Destiny Blueprint is more than just an academic exercise; it affects the depths of our emotions and souls, reawakening a feeling of wonder about the complexities of life and the destiny we each carry. It requires us to strike a fine balance between yielding to the flow of fate and actively altering the trajectory of our life.
Join us as we embark on this thought-provoking journey into the realm of The Destiny Blueprint, where the boundless mysteries of the human experience await exploration, contemplation, and perhaps a touch of revelation.

CHAPTER 1: UNDERSTANDING DESTINY AND DISCIPLINE

Defining Destiny

Destiny, the enigmatic power that weaves the fabric of our life, has always piqued the interest of human beings. It entices us with the promise of meaning, of a set route tailored to each person. But what precisely is destiny, and how does it influence our lives?

Destiny, at its core, is a great symphony of inevitability and free will dancing in unison. It is the result of decisions made, chances taken, and obstacles overcome. It is the concept that every step in our path serves a higher purpose, directing us to our real mission.

Some see destiny as an immutable script written in the stars, while others see it as a constantly shifting constellation sculpted by the ripples of our deeds. Whatever your point of view, destiny is a powerful force that demands contemplation and bravery.

Determining our destiny entails delving into the depths of our spirit, questioning the nature of our ambitions, and seeking congruence between our goals and deeds. It is a self-discovery journey in which we excavate the gems of our deepest passions and convictions.

Embracing destiny is embracing the power inside to realize aspirations and build a path of purpose rather than succumbing to fate. Rather than succumbing to complacency or circumstance, it is about appreciating the role of discipline and resilience in molding our futures.
In order to achieve success via discipline, we must accept that fate may lead us wrong or provide unexpected turns. Our determination is tested and our character is refined during these times of uncertainty.

As we navigate the ever-changing waves of life, we must remember that destiny is a journey, not a destination. It is the quest of personal development, excellence, and being the best version of oneself.

So, my traveler, whether you think fate is written or weaved, let us go on this journey together, unraveling the mysteries, embracing the obstacles, and reveling in the beauty of crafting our own destiny. Because, in the end, it is our decisions and the discipline we accept that open our life' limitless potential.

Embracing Discipline

Accepting discipline is like accepting the guiding hand that takes us to our actual potential. It is our constant companion on our path of self-improvement and progress. Discipline enables us to remain focused on our goals in the face of distractions and barriers.

Discipline is fundamentally the skill of self-control and constancy. It encourages us to make clear aims, develop a road map to our goals, and stick to it with zeal. We create habits that nurture our brains, bodies, and spirits via discipline, creating resilience and determination.

Accepting discipline necessitates confronting our faults and transforming them into strengths. It encourages us to push ourselves beyond of our comfort zones, to set goals for ourselves, and to strive for constant growth.

Discipline becomes the anchor that keeps us anchored in the face of hardship. It reminds us to keep going when the going gets tough, to get back up when we fall, and to learn from our errors.

Discipline develops a sense of duty and obligation toward others in addition to personal progress. It enhances our bonds and attracts the admiration of people around us.

Accepting discipline is a lifetime commitment to self-improvement. It opens the door to achievement, self-discovery, and fulfillment, revealing the tremendous potential that each of us possesses. So, let us welcome discipline with open arms, since it is the path to a life of purpose and success.

The Interplay between Destiny and Discipline
The interaction between fate and discipline is a profound and nuanced ballet that molds our life. It is a delicate balancing act between fate's guiding hand and an unrelenting devotion to self-improvement. Understanding this dynamic can help us embrace our path with purpose and drive as we negotiate life's twists and turns.

Destiny, which is sometimes viewed as a predetermined path, is the invisible force that guides us to specific chances and interactions. The coincidence of events, persons, and situations appears to be fortuitous, hinting to a larger plan. However, destiny is not a fixed blueprint; it is a dynamic and ever-changing process that reacts to our actions and decisions.

Discipline, on the other hand, is the propellant that drives us ahead on our journey. It is the practice of self-control, dedication, and constancy. We harness our willpower via discipline to stay focused on our goals even in the face of hardship. The steady hand changes our behaviors and habits, turning simple aspirations into practical reality.

Destiny gives us key moments and crossroads as we travel through life. These are chances to venture outside of our comfort zones, test our limitations, and welcome change. Discipline becomes our most useful ally at these vital junctures. The decisions we make and acts we take at these moments of fate affect the course of our life.

Consider Sarah, a young entrepreneur with a love for technology. Destiny takes her to a networking event, where she meets an experienced mentor who offers her an internship at a cutting-edge technology corporation. Destiny led her to this chance, but discipline will decide her success in it.

Sarah immerses herself in the internship, absorbing knowledge and improving her talents with unrelenting determination. She works tirelessly, trying to leave a lasting impression. Her perseverance leads her to overcome obstacles and disappointments, translating her potential into real-world knowledge.

As Sarah's internship comes to an end, fate intervenes once more, presenting her with two options: a job offer from the tech giant and an invitation to join a promising start-up. Destiny creates the scene, but it is her discipline that allows her to make an informed decision.

Sarah considers her long-term objectives and principles, weighing the implications of each decision. She selects the start-up with clarity of purpose, feeling it better resonates with her vision for innovation and autonomy. Her methodical approach to decision-making enables her to grab the opportunity that most aligns with her goals.

Destiny continues to weave its intricate patterns across our lives, providing unexpected twists and fortunate meetings. However, discipline serves as the weaver, weaving our actions and decisions into a unified tapestry. Our discipline dictates how we respond to destiny's call, whether we seize opportunities or let them pass through our fingers.

Destiny may sometimes bring us through difficult stages, putting our willpower and devotion to the test. Discipline becomes our anchor during these times, offering the strength to weather the storms and emerge stronger on the other side. It teaches us that excellence is earned by constant labor and patience, not overnight.

The interaction of destiny and discipline is a ballet of subtle complexity rather than a linear route. It is about accepting life's uncertainty while being devoted to our progress and ambitions. It reminds us that destiny is more than just getting to a goal; it is also about finding meaning in the trip itself.

The dance of destiny and discipline is one of harmony and balance. Destiny creates possibilities, but discipline is the driving force that makes those opportunities a reality. Embracing both components enables us to manage the complexities of life with elegance and purpose, revealing the incredible potential that everyone of us possesses.

CHAPTER 2: THE POWER OF VISION AND PURPOSE

Discovering Your True Vision

Finding your real vision is like uncovering a buried gem in the great expanse of life's journey. It is a fundamental journey that goes beyond objectives and desires, directing you towards a meaningful and fulfilled living. Your real vision serves as a guiding light, illuminating your path and directing your decisions, actions, and objectives. But how can one engage on this life-changing journey of self-discovery and reveal their genuine vision?

1. Examining One's Passions and Talents:
Introspection is the first step in discovering your actual vision. Consider your interests, the activities that pique your interest and offer you delight. What activities cause you to become disoriented about time? Identify your natural talents and abilities, those one-of-a-kind gifts that set you distinct. Discovering your interests

and abilities can provide vital insights into your genuine vision.

2. Encourage Curiosity and Exploration:
Curiosity is the driving force behind exploration. Be open to new experiences and a wide range of information. Participate in activities and interests that fascinate you, even if they appear unconnected to your current career. The more you investigate, the wider your horizons get and the closer you are to understanding your genuine vision.

3. Determining Values and Beliefs:
Your actual vision is inextricably linked to your values and beliefs. Consider what is most important to you in life, what beliefs you hold dear, and what legacy you want to leave behind. Your values act as a compass, directing you toward a vision that is true to your actual self.

4. Accepting Failure and Learning:
The road to realizing your actual vision is not without its challenges. Accept failure as a

chance to learn and progress. Mistakes bring significant lessons and help people become more self-aware. Every failure may lead you to a more real and purposeful vision.

5. Imagine Your Ideal Life:
Close your eyes and visualize yourself living your ideal life. What do you notice? What provides you happiness and fulfillment? Visualization may help you clarify your desires and construct a mental blueprint of your genuine vision. The more specific your vision, the more real it becomes.

6. Seeking Role Models for Insight:
Take inspiration from role models and individuals who have accepted their own vision. Read their biographies, listen to their interviews, and learn how they chose their paths. Their stories might provide vital lessons and insights as you go on your own self-discovery path.

7. Abandoning External Expectations:
External expectations and societal conventions might impair your perception. Accept the fortitude to reject cultural pressures and standards that do not reflect your actual self. Create your own route by following your true interests, passions, and ideals.

8. Accepting Mindfulness and Intuition:
Mindfulness practice and self-awareness cultivation can help you realize your actual vision. Pay attention to your intuition, the tiny whispers of your heart, as they frequently give significant insights and direction.

9. Surrounding Yourself with Complimentary Allies:
Seek out a supporting network of family, friends, or mentors who can encourage and inspire you. Share your adventure with others who believe in you and can provide helpful advice and support along the road.

10. Accepting the Journey:
Remember that uncovering your genuine vision is a lifelong journey, not a destination. Accept the process, be patient with yourself, and let your vision adapt as you change and grow.

Discovering your genuine vision is an exciting journey that necessitates self-reflection, curiosity, and an openness to life's possibilities. It is about bringing your passions, abilities, values, and beliefs together to create a life that is purpose-driven and meaningful. Embrace the trip with bravery and conviction, for it will lead you to the unique tapestry of your genuine vision, which will direct you to a life of meaning and influence.

Aligning Your Purpose with Destiny

Life is a lovely tapestry woven with strands of fate and meaning. Destiny, the enigmatic force that leads us to specific experiences and interactions, and purpose, the underlying reason for our being, are inextricably linked in a dance of interplay. Discovering and connecting your purpose with destiny is a life-changing adventure that provides clarity, fulfillment, and a feeling of belonging.

Accepting Self-Discovery: The first step in aligning your mission with destiny is to start on a self-discovery journey. Consider your interests, abilities, and values. Investigate your hopes and dreams. Consider the significant occasions in your life that influenced you. Introspection will help you uncover the core of your genuine mission.

Trusting Your Intuition: Our intuition is a delicate compass that steers us toward alignment with our destiny. Listen to your heart's whispers and trust your instincts. Our intuition frequently gives important insights that can lead us to opportunities and experiences that are in keeping with our purpose.

Recognizing Synchronicities: Be aware of synchronicities, which are significant coincidences that appear to be more than random happenings. These synchronicities might be signs from the universe directing you to your destiny. Be willing to recognize and comprehend their meaning.

Accepting Destiny's Unpredictability: Destiny is not always clear. It might take unforeseen twists and offer difficulties. Accept the unpredictability of fate with an open heart. The most profound growth and purpose-aligned opportunities can sometimes arise from the unexpected.

Gratitude Cultivation: Gratitude is a potent motivator for aligning with destiny. Even during difficult times, count your blessings and cherish the trip. Gratitude opens your heart to the bounty that life provides, allowing you to perceive the opportunities that await you.

Limiting Beliefs: Limiting beliefs can make it difficult to align with your mission and destiny. Replace any beliefs that no longer serve you with powerful ones. Accept the idea that you are meant for greatness and that your goal is worthwhile to pursue.

Setting Intentions: Set intentions that are congruent with your goal. Immerse yourself in the emotions connected with attaining your purpose-aligned objectives by visualizing your desired results. Intentions work like a magnet, attracting chances that align with your real calling.

Accepting Growth and Evolution: Your mission and destiny do not remain static; they change as you develop and learn. Accept personal development and lifelong learning. Your purpose may change as you grow, and your destiny may blossom in unforeseen ways. Allow for this wonderful growth.

Serving Others: Aligning your mission with destiny frequently entails some form of service to others. Consider how your particular talents and interests might benefit the well-being of others. A life of purpose is frequently connected with actions of kindness, compassion, and community service.

Trust in Divine Timing: Have faith in the notion of divine timing. There may be times when it appears that your mission is not progressing as rapidly as you would want. Believe that fate has its own timetable, and that the parts will fall into place at the right time.

Aligning your purpose with destiny is a deep and transformational path of self-discovery, faith, and receptivity to life's chances. Accept the interaction between destiny and purpose, understanding that by listening to your intuition, setting empowered intentions, and following your heart, the way to harmony becomes apparent. You will experience a synergy between destiny and your greatest goals as you align with your true purpose, producing a life of fulfillment, meaning, and influence. Embrace the beauty of this trip, for it is a dance with destiny that will lead you to live a life of purpose and realizing your full potential.

Crafting a Compelling Life Mission

A compelling life mission functions as a guiding light in the broad canvas of life, illuminating the route towards a purposeful and fulfilled living. It's a declaration of purpose that encapsulates the core of who you are, what you stand for, and the influence you want to make on the world. Making a compelling life goal is a life-changing activity that gives clarity, concentration, and alignment to your journey.

1. **Examine Your Values and interests:** Understanding your underlying values and interests is the cornerstone of a compelling life goal. Take some time to consider what is genuinely important to you in life. Determine the activities that energize your spirit and the causes that touch your heart. Your beliefs and interests will serve as the foundation for your life mission.

2. **Define Your Purpose:** Your life mission is an extension of your purpose, which is the fundamental reason for your being. Consider your desired effect on the world and the legacy

you intend to leave behind. What do you hope to contribute to society? Define your objective clearly and intentionally.

3. **Identify Your Strengths:** Your individual strengths and abilities are critical in developing a compelling life goal. Recognize your natural strengths and places where you thrive. Use these assets to power your purpose and make a significant difference.

4. **Visualize Your Ideal existence:** Close your eyes and imagine your ideal existence. Consider living in accordance with your purpose, values, and interests. Visualize the difference you're making, the joy you're having, and the fulfillment you're getting from fulfilling your goal. Allow this vision to inspire and guide you as you develop your life's goal.

5. **Create a Clear and short phrase:** In order to create a compelling life mission, you must condense your purpose and vision into a clear and short phrase. Your mission statement should be a strong statement of desire and the change you want to see. Keep it simple yet powerful, and make sure it speaks to your heart.

6. **Make It Actionable:** A compelling life mission is more than a declaration; it is a call to action. Infuse practical language into your purpose that encourages and enables you to take concrete efforts toward its fulfillment. Use verbs and phrases that convey resolve and purpose.

7. **Align with Your actual Self:** Your life goal should be in line with your actual self, which is the most honest representation of who you are. Avoid creating a mission based on society standards or external expectations. Accept your own individuality and allow it to come through in your purpose.

8. **Establish Meaningful objectives:** Your life mission acts as a compass for establishing meaningful objectives. Determine short-term and long-term goals that are in line with your mission. Each target you select should contribute to the overall success of your mission.

9. **Take Inspired Action:** A compelling life purpose is not a passive pronouncement; it necessitates inspired action on your part. Align your everyday activities, decisions, and choices with your objective. Allow your goal to be the

driving force that pulls you ahead into a life of meaning and influence.

Making a compelling life mission is a reflective and transforming process that gives clarity, concentration, and alignment to your journey. You may construct a strong statement that encompasses the core of who you are and the effect you want to make by focusing on your beliefs, interests, and purpose. Accept your mission's call to action and allow it to lead you to a life of significance, fulfillment, and authenticity. You will find yourself living a fascinating and purposeful life as you link your activities with your goal, making a positive impression on the world around you.

CHAPTER 3: CULTIVATING SELF - DISCIPLINE

Building Strong Habits

Habits are the foundation of our everyday life. They influence our actions, habits, and, eventually, our fate. Building strong habits is a life-changing process that allows us to make good changes, achieve our objectives, and live a more satisfying life. Strong habits lay the path for long-term success, whether it's adopting healthier routines, increasing productivity, or building a growth mentality. Here are some basic tactics for developing and sustaining solid habits.

Begin Small and Stay persistent: The key to developing powerful habits is to begin small and stay persistent. Begin with activities that are attainable and manageable in relation to your goals. Consistency is essential since it maintains the habit loop in our minds. When you repeatedly perform a behavior, it becomes easier over time and develops a strong habit.

Establish explicit and quantifiable Goals: Clearly identify the behaviors you wish to develop and create explicit, quantifiable goals. Goals that are either vague or too broad make it difficult to measure progress and stay motivated. Divide your goals into tiny milestones and celebrate each one along the road.

Establish a schedule: Create a daily or weekly schedule that combines the habit you wish to develop. Having a defined timetable makes incorporating the new behavior into your life simpler. Practicing the habit at the same time and location every day reinforces its relevance in your daily routine.

Remove Distractions and Barriers: Reduce distractions and eliminate temptations that may impede your habit-building process. Create an atmosphere that encourages your desired behavior and removes any roadblocks to achievement. For example, if you want to read more books, have a book nearby and limit distractions such as mobile gadgets.

Monitor Your Progress: Keep track of your habit-building progress. Keep a habit tracker, notepad, or digital tool to document your daily success. Seeing your accomplishments and progress may motivate you and reaffirm the positive adjustments you are making.

Maintain Accountability: Accountability is a key tool for developing strong habits. Discuss your objectives with a friend, family member, or a support group. Having someone to keep you responsible and support you can help you stay on track, especially during difficult times.

Recognize the Power of Repetition: Habits are formed via repetition. The more you do something, the more it becomes engrained in your daily life. The behavior becomes habitual with time, needing less work and energy to continue.

Be Patient and Kind to Yourself: Developing good habits takes time. Be kind with yourself and recognize that setbacks are a normal part of the process. Instead of berating yourself for little blunders, practice self-compassion and concentrate on getting back on track.

Developing good habits is a great instrument for personal development and achievement. You may create behaviors that correspond with your goals by starting small, being consistent, and having clear goals. Remember to keep track of your development and to believe in the power of repetition. Be kind with yourself and rejoice in each step forward. You can change your behaviors and live a more pleasant and purposeful life if you work hard enough.

Overcoming Procrastination
Procrastination, or the act of deferring or postponing chores and obligations, is a frequent challenge that many people experience. It frequently leaves us dissatisfied, anxious, and

unproductive. Overcoming procrastination requires self-awareness, discipline, and a transformation in perspective. We may break free from procrastination's grasp and embrace a life of activity and productivity by recognizing the core causes of procrastination and using effective techniques.

Understanding Procrastination's Root Causes
A lot of things can contribute to procrastination. Fear of failure, perfectionism, a lack of drive, and overload are all major contributors to procrastination. Recognizing the reasons for procrastination is the first step toward conquering it.

1. Failure worry: The worry of failing to fulfill expectations or making mistakes can freeze us into inaction. It puts a barrier between us and our goals, causing us to put off taking the essential measures.

2. Perfectionism: The pursuit of perfection may be a double-edged sword. While it motivates us

to achieve our best, it may also stymie progress as we wait for the "perfect" time to begin or complete a work.

3. Lack of Motivation: When we lack interest or excitement for a work, it is difficult to begin or continue our efforts, which leads to procrastination.

4. Feeling overwhelmed by the sheer number of duties or the intricacy of a project can lead to avoidance and procrastination.

Effective Strategies to Overcome Procrastination

1. Establish Clear and Specific Goals: Divide your work into smaller, more attainable goals. Set firm deadlines and prioritize them based on their relevance. Specific goals give clarity and direction, making action simpler.

2. Create a Routine: Creating a daily or weekly routine can aid in the creation of structure and

discipline. Maintain a timetable that includes time for work, breaks, and leisure.

3. Use Time Management strategies: Use time management strategies such as the Pomodoro Technique, which involves working in small, concentrated intervals separated by brief breaks. This increases productivity and decreases feelings of overload.

4. Begin with a tiny Step: When confronted with a difficult undertaking, begin with a tiny, manageable portion of it. This can assist to generate momentum and lessen perceived effort, making it simpler to keep going.

5. Develop a Growth Mindset: Accept the concept that mistakes and failures may be used to learn and progress. Focus on progress rather than perfection, and see obstacles as opportunities for growth.

6. Reduce Distractions: Identify and eliminate potential distractions in your surroundings. Turn

off alerts, choose a workplace, and prioritize focusing on the task at hand.

7. Establish Boundaries: Learn to say no to extra obligations that might stymie your progress on vital objectives. Setting limits safeguards your time and energy.

8. Reward Yourself: Recognize and appreciate your accomplishments, no matter how minor. Rewarding oneself for activities completed can promote positive behaviors and drive you to keep going.

9. Seek Accountability: Discuss your objectives with a friend, mentor, or coworker who can hold you responsible. Accountability may offer support and encouragement during difficult times.

Changing Your Procrastination Mindset
Overcoming procrastination necessitates not only the use of external solutions, but also a modification in our thinking. Here are some

strategies for overcoming procrastination and developing a proactive attitude to tasks:

1. Concentrate on the Advantages of Taking Action: Remind yourself of the benefits of finishing assignments on time. Consider the sense of success and stress reduction that comes with being proactive.

2. Use Visualization: Visualize yourself actively involved in the activity, feeling driven, and accomplishing it effectively. Visualization might help you feel more confident and less hesitant.

3. Follow the 2-Minute Rule: If a work can be completed in less than two minutes, do it right away. By handling little things as soon as possible, you build a sensation of accomplishment that pulls you ahead.

4. Design an Inspiring workstation: Create a workstation that inspires creativity and productivity. Surround yourself with objects and decorations that inspire you to act.

5. Monitor Your Self-Talk: Be mindful of any negative self-talk that is feeding your procrastination. Replace negative self-talk with uplifting and helpful words.

6. Create a Mantra: Create a mantra or affirmation that reminds you of your skills and motivates you to take action. When you sense the impulse to postpone, repeat that to yourself.

7. Practice Gratitude: Be grateful for the opportunity to complete things and improve. Gratitude changes your attention away from what you "have to" do and toward what you "get to" accomplish.

8. Reflect on prior Experiences: Consider prior instances of procrastination and uncover trends or causes. Use these findings to develop future success tactics.

9. Seek Inspiration: Surround yourself with people that have a proactive mentality, and draw

inspiration from their tales and accomplishments.

10. Celebrate Progress: Celebrate any and every progress you achieve. Recognize that each step forward is a success in the battle against procrastination.

Overcoming procrastination is a path that needs self-awareness, discipline, and a mental transformation. We may break free from procrastination's grasp and embrace a life of activity and productivity by recognizing the core causes of procrastination and using effective techniques. To overcome the obstacles of procrastination, create clear objectives, adopt routines, and cultivate a growth mentality. Remember to be patient with yourself, to be compassionate to yourself, and to celebrate your success along the road. Accepting action and productivity will result in a more satisfying and fulfilled existence.

Nurturing Mental Resilience

In the face of adversity, cultivating mental resilience is essential for bouncing back, adapting, and prospering. The capacity to cope with stress, disappointments, and hardship while having a positive view is referred to as mental resilience. It is a skill that can be developed and improved via deliberate practices and mindset modifications. Here are some ways for developing mental resilience:

Develop a Growth mentality: Adopt a growth mentality in which obstacles are viewed as opportunities for learning and progress. Consider setbacks to be temporary roadblocks rather than permanent failures. In order to recognize that talents and abilities may be acquired through time, emphasize progress and effort.

Practice Self-Compassion: Be kind and understanding to yourself, even when things are tough. Avoid negative self-talk and self-criticism. Treat yourself with the same kindness and understanding that you would show to a friend who is going through a difficult time.

Develop Optimism: Develop an optimistic attitude on life by concentrating on the positives and potential rather than the downsides. Look for silver linings in difficult situations and keep a positive mindset.

Create a Supportive Network: Surround yourself with encouraging friends, relatives, or mentors who can lend a listening ear during difficult times. Social support may be a potent antidote to stress and misfortune.

Identify Healthy Coping techniques: Identify healthy coping techniques that work for you, such as mindfulness, exercise, writing, or hobbies. Use these tactics on a regular basis to strengthen your resilience in the face of stress.

Set Achievable and reasonable objectives: Set attainable and reasonable objectives for yourself. Break down huge activities into smaller, more manageable chunks, and remember to celebrate each milestone along the way. This strategy promotes a sense of achievement and drive.

Challenge Negative ideas: Replace negative ideas with more positive and inspiring ones. Reframing negative thought patterns aids in the development of a more resilient attitude.

Learn from hardship: Look for possibilities for development and lessons in the face of hardship. Consider how you overcame obstacles in the past and apply what you learned to present issues.

Mental resilience is developed via deliberate self-care, attitude development, and learning to negotiate life's ups and downs. Mental resilience may be built through building a growth attitude, practicing self-compassion, and nurturing optimism. Building mental strength also involves surrounding oneself with helpful people, using healthy coping mechanisms, and setting realistic objectives. Remember that cultivating mental resilience requires flexibility, attention, and finding purpose in life. Most essential, if you want expert assistance, do not hesitate to get it. By using these tactics, you may become more resilient, better able to deal with life's problems, and embrace a more rewarding and empowered way of life.

CHAPTER 4:TIME MANAGEMENT FOR SUCCESS

Prioritizing Your Goals

In today's fast-paced and demanding environment, it's critical to prioritize our goals in order to stay focused and achieve what genuinely matters to us. Prioritization is making deliberate decisions and devoting our time, energy, and resources to the most important pursuits. We may develop a roadmap for success and fulfillment by defining our most essential goals and organizing them in a meaningful sequence. Here are some techniques for properly prioritizing your goals:

Identify Your Core Values and Vision:

Begin by considering your basic principles and long-term life goals. What is genuinely important to you? Understanding your beliefs and vision lays the groundwork for aligning your ambitions with your true self.

Establish Specific and Measurable Objectives:

To eliminate ambiguity and vagueness, make your goals explicit and quantifiable. Define your goals clearly and develop quantifiable criteria to measure your success. Specific objectives provide you with a clear sense of direction and allow you to appreciate accomplishments along the way.

Determine the Impact and Alignment:

Examine the impact of each aim and its connection with your values and vision. Consider the repercussions of accomplishing or failing to achieve each goal. Prioritize objectives that will have a major beneficial influence on your life and that are thoroughly aligned with your beliefs.

Think about Time Sensitivity:

When prioritizing your goals, keep time constraints in mind. Some goals may have deadlines or precise time limits that must be met right away, but others may be more flexible. To prevent extra strain and stress, prioritize time-sensitive goals first.

Apply the Pareto Principle:
According to the Pareto Principle, often known as the 80/20 rule, 80% of the results come from 20% of the work. Apply this idea to your objectives by concentrating on the 20% of your goals that have the most influence and result in the most significant outcomes.

Be Prepared to Let Go:
Recognize that you may need to let go of certain ambitions in order to focus on what is genuinely important. We can sometimes overextend ourselves by chasing too many goals. Allow yourself to say no to non-essential ambitions in order to make room for what actually resonates with your vision.

Make self-care and well-being a priority:
Remember to emphasize self-care and well-being while creating goals. It is critical to

maintain your physical and mental health in order to maintain attention, energy, and productivity. In order to refuel and stay motivated, incorporate self-care routines into your daily routine.

Review and adjust on a regular basis:
Prioritization is a continuous process. Review your objectives on a regular basis, analyze your progress, and alter your priorities as appropriate. Life is fluid, and circumstances may shift. As you develop and change, be adaptive and open to modifying your goals.

Prioritizing your objectives is a critical step in achieving attention, productivity, and contentment. You may construct a success roadmap by articulating your values and vision, creating precise targets, and analyzing impact and alignment. To make educated judgments, consider time sensitivity, dependencies, and available resources. Accept the Pareto Principle and be willing to let go of non-essential ambitions in order to focus on the most significant goals. Make self-care a priority in order to preserve general well-being and productivity. As your life changes, examine and update your priorities on a regular basis. By implementing these tactics, you may create a life that is centered on your most essential goals, giving you a feeling of purpose and achievement. Remember that it is not about doing more; it is about doing what is most important to you.

Eliminating Time-Wasting Activities

In our fast-paced world, time is a vital resource. Unfortunately, we frequently waste significant time on activities that do not contribute to our goals or well-being. These time-wasters not only reduce production but also raise tension and frustration. To make the most of our days, we must identify and remove time wasters. By doing so, we may make room for more important and productive activities. Here are some time-wasting ways to help you remove them and create more productive days:

Identify Your Time-Wasters: Begin by recognizing activities that take up a substantial amount of your time yet produce no meaningful outcomes. Excessive social media scrolling, excessive television viewing, gossiping, and idle internet surfing are all common time wasters.

Establish Clear Priorities: Define your priorities and match your efforts with your aims and values. When you have a clear sense of what is most important to you, it is easy to identify activities that do not contribute to your growth and well-being.

Create a Time Audit: For a few days, do a time audit to track how you spend your time. Keep track of your activities and how much time you devote to each. The time audit will show patterns and indicate areas where you may be more efficient with your time.

Set Technology Boundaries: If not utilized carefully, technology can be a big time waster. Set limits by shutting off unneeded notifications, scheduling certain times to read emails, and limiting distractions with applications or website blockers.

Delegate and Say No: Accept that you cannot accomplish everything on your own. When appropriate, delegate duties to others and learn to say no to obligations that do not line with your priorities.
Breaking activities into smaller, achievable stages might help you avoid feeling overwhelmed and delayed. Concentrate on taking one step at a time and celebrating your accomplishments along the way.

Plan Your Day: Make a daily plan or to-do list to help you arrange your day and dedicate time to the most critical things. A strategy helps you stay focused and decreases the probability of engaging in pointless activity.

Reduce Multitasking: Multitasking can reduce productivity and cause mistakes. Concentrate on one activity at a time and give it your undivided attention before moving on to the next.

Cultivate a healthy Relationship with Time: Develop a healthy, conscious relationship with time. Recognize its worth and make good use of it. Consider time to be an important asset, and be deliberate about how you use it.

Take Regular pauses: It may appear contradictory, but taking regular pauses can boost productivity. Breaks help you to refuel and refocus when you return to your responsibilities.

Allocate separate Time Blocks for Non-Essential Activities: Allocate separate time blocks for non-essential activities such as socializing or leisure. Setting boundaries ensures that you have time for these hobbies while not allowing them to consume your whole day.

Eliminating time-wasting tasks is a game changer for unlocking more productive days and reaching your goals. You get insight into how you spend your time by identifying time wasters, creating clear priorities, and performing a time audit. To maximize your time utilization, practice conscious consumption, create boundaries with technology, and avoid pointless meetings. To improve attention and efficiency, divide jobs into smaller chunks, plan your day, and avoid multitasking. Develop a healthy connection with time by taking frequent breaks and limiting time spent on non-essential tasks. Minimalism may help you establish a clutter-free atmosphere that supports your priorities. You can reclaim your time, enhance productivity, and live a more conscious and satisfying life by applying these tactics.

CHAPTER 5: DISCIPLINE IN GOAL SETTING

Setting S.M.A.R.T. Goals

Setting goals is a powerful process that allows us to make our hopes and aspirations a reality. But not all objectives are created equal. To maximize our chances of success, we must create S.M.A.R.T. Goals that are Specific, Measurable, Achievable, Relevant, and Time-bound are known as S.M.A.R.T. goals. This widely utilized framework serves as a road map for success, assisting us in remaining focused, motivated, and on track. Here's how to set S.M.A.R.T. objectives:

Specific: Define Your Goal Clearly

Making a S.M.A.R.T. goal explicit and well-defined is the first stage. Avoid making broad or generic generalizations. Your route to success will be clearer if you are more explicit.

A non-specific objective would be, "I want to improve my fitness."

S.M.A.R.T. goal example: "I want to run a 5-kilometer race in six months, improving my current running time by 20%."

Measurable: Monitor Your Progress

A quantifiable objective enables you to measure your progress and identify when you've reached your goal. Include specific criteria for measuring your achievement. Make your aim as quantifiable as possible by quantifying it. You'll know exactly how far you've come and what you need to accomplish to attain your goal this way.

A non-measurable aim would be, "I want to be better at time management."

A quantifiable S.M.A.R.T. objective may be something like, "I want to spend at least 30 minutes each day on focused work to complete my project by the deadline."

Achievable: Establish Realistic Goals

A reasonable aim is one that you can achieve given your resources, talents, and circumstances. While pushing oneself is vital, establishing unachievable objectives can lead to frustration and disappointment. When deciding on a goal, consider your present talents and resources.

Unachievable goal: "I want to be a professional musician despite having no prior musical experience."

Example of an S.M.A.R.T. goal: "I want to take guitar lessons for six months and be able to play three songs proficiently by the end of the period."

Relevant: Align with your values and goals.

A relevant aim is one that is consistent with your beliefs, aspirations, and long-term goals. It should be relevant and beneficial to your personal or professional development. Make sure your objective is important to you and worth the effort and time you put into it.

Irrelevant goal: "I want to learn to knit, despite having no interest in it.

An appropriate S.M.A.R.T. objective may be, "I want to improve my public speaking skills so that I can confidently present my ideas during team meetings at work."

Time-bound: Establish a Deadline
A time-bound goal has a fixed completion date. This sense of urgency instills accountability in you and drives you to take persistent action. Set a realistic schedule for completing your objective, and if required, break it down into smaller stages.
"I want to write a book someday," for example, is an example of a goal with no timeframe.
A time-bound S.M.A.R.T. goal may be, "I'd like to finish the first draft of my work in three months by writing at least 500 words every week."

Setting S.M.A.R.T. goals is an effective method for obtaining success in a variety of domains. You build a clear roadmap to follow by making your goals Specific, Measurable, Achievable, Relevant, and Time-bound. Remember to define your goals specifically, to develop quantifiable criteria, to set realistic targets, to assure relevancy, and to set clear timeframes. S.M.A.R.T. objectives keep you focused, motivated, and on track, bringing you closer to your hopes and aspirations.

Staying Focused on Your Objectives

Staying focused on our goals is a difficult but necessary challenge in our fast-paced and often chaotic life. Distractions, unanticipated occurrences, and conflicting goals can easily derail us off our success path. Maintaining concentration, on the other hand, is critical for reaching our objectives and realizing our ambitions. Here are some excellent ways for staying focused on your goals and increasing your chances of success:

Define Your Goals Clearly

The first step toward staying focused is to clearly define your goals. Define what you want to accomplish and why it is important to you. Having a strong and meaningful "why" may give the inspiration and drive you need to stay focused during difficult circumstances.

Divide Your Objectives Into Milestones

Large, long-term goals can be daunting, resulting in a loss of concentration. Divide your goals into smaller, more manageable benchmarks. These modest stages provide you a clear route ahead, allowing you to enjoy little victories while maintaining momentum.

Organize Your Tasks

Not all tasks are equally vital in meeting your goals. Prioritize your to-do list according to the importance of the tasks and their connection with your goals. Prioritize high-priority jobs first, then move on to less essential ones.

Reduce Distractions

Identify and eliminate distractions that may cause you to deviate from your goals. Turn off unneeded alerts, keep your workplace orderly, and set limits with coworkers and family members to create a conducive work atmosphere.

Improve Your Time Management Skills
Effective time management is critical for remaining on track with your goals. Prioritize work, delegate if possible, and prevent procrastinating. To improve attention and productivity, use time management strategies such as the Pomodoro Technique.

Accept Mindfulness and Meditation
Mindfulness and meditation practice can help you stay focused and present. These routines increase attention span and decrease mind wandering, helping you to focus on your goals more efficiently.

Develop Self-Discipline
Staying focused necessitates self-discipline and the capacity to reject temptations that lead you astray. Set limits, stick to your plan, and keep yourself accountable to practice self-discipline.

Imagine Your Success

Visualization is an effective method for maintaining attention and motivation. Visualize yourself reaching your goals and reaping the benefits of your efforts on a regular basis. This positive reinforcement maintains your goals in front of your mind.

Setbacks provide us valuable lessons.

Accept that setbacks are a normal part of the process of accomplishing your goals. Rather of allowing failures to disrupt your concentration, use them as chances for learning and progress. Analyze what went wrong, modify your strategy, and proceed with fresh zeal.

Examine and Make Changes Regularly

Review your goals and progress on a regular basis. Examine whether your objectives are still relevant and, if so, revise them. Regular assessments ensure that you remain focused on what is genuinely important and that you adjust to changing circumstances.

Take Good Care of Yourself

Finally, don't disregard your well-being in the pursuit of your goals. Take care of your physical and mental health in order to preserve focus and vitality. To maximize your effectiveness, prioritize proper rest, exercise, and self-care.

Maintaining concentration on your goals is a critical ability for achieving success and contentment. Define your goals clearly, divide them into milestones, and prioritize your work. Make a daily plan, establish S.M.A.R.T. goals, and keep distractions to a minimum. Accept awareness, develop self-discipline, and imagine your accomplishment. Seek help and responsibility, learn from setbacks, and remain optimistic. Review and alter your goals on a regular basis, and emphasize your well-being. By adopting these tactics into your everyday life, you will be able to stay focused on your goals, negotiate adversities with resilience, and strive toward your goals. Remember that the road to success is frequently a marathon, not a sprint, so being focused and persevering are essential.

CHAPTER 6: THE ROLE OF PERSEVERANCE

Overcoming Obstacles and Setbacks

Life is a journey full of ups and downs, victories and failures, triumphs and challenges. Setbacks and obstacles are unavoidable on this road. While they may be depressing, they also provide possibilities for development, learning, and resilience building. How we respond to these challenges determines our capacity to overcome them and continue on the path to success. In this essay, we will discuss the significance of overcoming barriers and failures, the mentality required to do so, and successful tactics for transforming setbacks into stepping stones toward victory.

Overcoming Obstacles and Setbacks is Critical

Obstacles and disappointments are unavoidable in life. They might appear as unanticipated failures, financial troubles, health concerns, marital difficulties, or job setbacks. While it is natural to feel dejected or defeated when confronted with such challenges, it is critical to recognize that conquering them is an important element of personal growth and development.

1. **Developing Resilience:** Resilience is the ability to recover from adversity, adapt, and persevere in the face of failures. Taking on challenges enables us to develop resilience. We grow better equipped to face future problems with courage and calm by learning to persist in the face of adversity.

2. **Character Building:** Overcoming problems puts our character and integrity to the test. It displays our genuine values and beliefs. Our character is defined by how we deal with setbacks and the decisions we make. Accepting obstacles with bravery and commitment allows us to become a stronger, more real character.

3. **Developing Wisdom:** Each hurdle and failure teaches us something new. We can get insights

into our behaviors, decisions, and cognitive processes through self-reflection and introspection. These lessons become priceless wisdom that helps us make better decisions in the future.

4. **Achieving Success:** Success is rarely a straight road. Most successful people have had multiple failures along the road. Overcoming hurdles with patience and resilience lays the route for eventual achievement. It enables us to fine-tune our goals, tactics, and approach, boosting our chances of success.

5. **Inspiring those:** Our capacity to overcome problems might serve as an example to those who are facing similar issues. We may bring hope and encouragement to people in need by sharing our tales of perseverance and victory, establishing a sense of community and support.

The Mindset Required to Overcome Obstacles and Setbacks

Having the appropriate perspective is essential for overcoming challenges and failures. Our attitude influences how we respond to situations by shaping our ideas, emotions, and behaviors. The following attitude attributes are required for overcoming obstacles:

1. Positivity: Maintain an optimistic attitude, viewing challenges as chances for progress rather than impassable barriers. Rather of focusing on the bad, emphasize the possibilities and potential solutions.

2. Perseverance: Adopt a never-say-die mentality. Recognize that progress may be slow and that setbacks are only temporary. Regardless of the barriers that arise, keep pushing forward, one step at a time.

3. Adaptability: Be adaptive and open to change. Life is dynamic, and things might change suddenly. Being adaptable in your approach helps you to make adjustments and find alternate routes to your goals.

4. Acceptance: Recognize that setbacks are a natural part of life and that you cannot control everything. Acceptance allows you to let go of unneeded resistance and focus on what you have control over.

5. Self-Belief: Have faith in your own talents and potential. Believe in your ability to solve problems and make sound judgments. Self-belief allows you to confront obstacles with confidence.

6. Growth attitude: Adopt a growth attitude, viewing setbacks and failures as chances for learning and advancement. Consider obstacles as opportunities to learn new talents and hone old ones.

Effective Ways to Overcome Obstacles and Setbacks
While difficulties may appear to be insurmountable, they are not. We may overcome failures and emerge stronger and more motivated

to attain our goals by utilizing successful strategies:

1. Reframe the Situation: Positively reframe the impediment to change your viewpoint on it. Instead of viewing it as a hindrance, consider it a diversion that might lead to new chances and experiences.

2. Break Down the Obstacle: When confronted with a difficult challenge, break it down into smaller, more doable tasks. This method helps you focus on doable milestones, making the project feel less daunting.

3. Seek Help: Seek help and encouragement from friends, family, and mentors. Discussing your problems with others might bring significant insights and emotional support.

4. Learn from Setbacks: Spend time analyzing setbacks and identifying the lessons they provide. Learning from your failures allows you

to avoid making the same mistakes in the future and make better decisions.

5. Improve Problem-Solving Skills: Develop problem-solving abilities so that you may tackle problems with a solution-oriented perspective.

6. Stay Committed to Your Goals: Remind yourself of your long-term goals and why they are important to you. Maintaining a strong commitment to your goals will help you stay motivated through difficult times.

7. Practice Self-Care: It is critical to take care of your physical and emotional well-being through difficult times. Make sure you get adequate rest, eat healthily, and do things that make you happy and relax.

8. Visualize Success: Visualization is an effective method for increasing motivation and attention. Visualize yourself effectively overcoming the impediment and accomplishing your goals on a regular basis. This mental

rehearsal might boost your confidence in your abilities to achieve.

9. Seek Inspiration: Read about others who have faced comparable challenges and succeeded. Hearing their experiences can inspire you and teach you about the tenacity required to overcome obstacles.

10. Embrace the Process: Instead of focusing simply on the destination, emphasize the journey. Recognize that regardless of the end, development and learning occur along the route. Overcoming hurdles and failures is an essential aspect of the path to success and personal development.

Developing Grit and Determination
We frequently face hurdles, disappointments, and times of uncertainty when pursuing our dreams and ambitions. Developing tenacity and drive are critical during these trying times. Grit is a blend of desire and perseverance, whereas determination is an unyielding determination to

attain our goals. These characteristics combine to generate a tremendous force that allows us to stay focused, endure adversity, and eventually achieve. In this article, we will look at the definition and significance of grit and determination, as well as the traits of gritty people and ways for cultivating these important attributes in our life.

Understanding Determination and Grit

Angela Duckworth, a psychologist, popularized the term grit, which she describes as the capacity to retain effort and enthusiasm in long-term goals despite setbacks, failures, and obstacles. It entails a strong feeling of purpose and a steady dedication to attaining one's goals. Determination, on the other hand, is the steadfast resolve to endure and push forward in the face of hurdles or problems. It is our inner power that keeps us going and stops us from giving up on our aspirations.

Grit and determination are both attributes that push people to achievement, assisting them in navigating life's inevitable ups and downs. They are the driving forces behind accomplishments that others may have thought were unattainable. Gritty and determined people have an uncommon level of tenacity, perseverance, and self-discipline that distinguishes them from those who succumb to adversity.

The Importance of Tenacity and Persistence

1. **Resilience:** The capacity to bounce back from losses and tackle difficulties with courage requires grit and commitment. Failures are viewed as chances for growth and learning by resilient people, helping them to adapt and endure in challenging situations.

2. **Long-Term objectives:** Achieving long-term objectives takes consistent effort and devotion. Gritty and determined people have the patience and tenacity to stick to their goals for long periods of time.

3. **Overcoming Adversities:** There are many uncertainties and adversities in life. Individuals with grit and drive may tackle issues straight on, finding answers and keeping focused on their

goals even in the face of enormous circumstances.

4. **Self-Motivation:** Determined and hardworking people have great self-motivation. They are not simply motivated by external recognition or incentives; instead, they find inner drive in the pursuit of their hobbies.

5. **Mental Toughness:** Grit and determination contribute to mental toughness, which is the capacity to retain attention, calm, and positivity under stress and pressure. Mental toughness is required for peak performance and success.

6. **Character Development:** Developing grit and drive promotes character development. These characteristics foster honesty, persistence, and discipline, transforming individuals into strong, principled leaders.

Strategies for Increasing Grit and Determination

1. Develop a Clear Vision: Create a clear vision of your long-term objectives and why they are essential to you. A strong sense of purpose will

offer the drive required to persevere during difficult circumstances.

2. Establish S.M.A.R.T. goals: Set goals that are specific, measurable, attainable, relevant, and time-bound. By breaking down huge goals into smaller, concrete actions, you may make them more manageable and feasible.

3. Accept obstacles: View obstacles as chances for development and learning. Accept setbacks as normal and transient, and see them as stepping stones in your journey.

4. Maintain Effort: Maintain persistent effort, even when improvement appears slow. Remember that even modest movements forward bring you closer to your objective.

5. Increase Resilience: Increase your resilience by adopting a positive attitude and employing coping skills such as mindfulness and self-reflection. Accept the notion that you can recover from failures stronger than before.

6. Seek Support and Accountability: Surround yourself with people who believe in your skills and encourage you when things become tough.

Seeking help and accountability from others might help you stay motivated.

7. Extract Lessons from Failures: Rather than concentrating on failures, extract lessons from them. Examine what went wrong, find areas for improvement, and modify your strategy appropriately.

9. Be Flexible and Adaptable: Be open to making changes and accepting change. Adaptability is necessary for growth when the route to achievement requires recalibration.

10. Overcome Setbacks: When confronted with a setback, dig deep and find the fortitude to endure. Continue to remind yourself of the importance of your long-term vision.

CHAPTER 7: BALANCING DISCIPLINE AND FLEXIBILITY

Adapting to Changing Circumstances

Change is unavoidable in life. We frequently experience unforeseen events in our personal and professional lives that force us to adapt and progress. Adapting to changing circumstances is more than simply a survival skill; it is a sign of perseverance and a road to success. This article discusses the importance of adapting to change, the advantages it provides, and techniques for developing this important life skill.

Understanding the Evolution of Change:

In life, change is unavoidable. Change is all around us, from little everyday variations to life-changing occurrences. Changes in relationships, job pathways, economic situations, health, and technology are all examples of how it might emerge. The capacity to negotiate these transitions with grace and flexibility is critical for personal growth and success.

The Value of Adaptability:
Adaptability is a crucial characteristic that distinguishes successful individuals and businesses from the competition. It is the ability to adapt, change, and prosper in a variety of settings. Stagnation, dissatisfaction, and wasted opportunities can result from a lack of adaptation. Those who welcome change, on the other hand, are more able to deal with obstacles, learn from experiences, and discover inventive solutions.

Advantages of Adapting to Change:
Resilience: The capacity to bounce back from setbacks and face adversity with fortitude and drive is fostered through adapting to changing circumstances. Individuals that are resilient are better able to deal with stress, preserve emotional well-being, and recover from life's adversities.

Life is full of ups and downs, and our resilience is tested in the face of adversity. Adaptable people recognize that obstacles are a part of the human experience and do not shy away from tackling them. Instead, they cultivate the mental toughness to overcome adversity, bounce back, and emerge stronger than before.

Personal Growth and Development: Embracing change promotes ongoing learning and personal development. When presented with new conditions, we are compelled to leave our comfort zones, learn new skills, and widen our horizons.

Consider the case of a professional who has spent years in the same field. With the rapid growth of technology, their career may become obsolete, or new chances in various industries may appear. To adapt to this shift, you must be willing to learn new skills and seek other job choices. Individuals find hidden abilities and hobbies they may not have realized existed via this process of continual learning, leading to a more meaningful existence.

Creativity and Innovation: Change frequently involves the development of new approaches to issues. Adaptable people are more imaginative and ingenious in their search for answers, which leads to growth and breakthroughs in a variety of disciplines.

In an atmosphere that supports experimentation and adaptability, innovation thrives. Businesses that welcome change and build an adaptive culture are more likely to stay ahead of the competition. Employees are encouraged to discuss new ideas, take measured risks, and accept failure as a crucial part of the learning process. This flexibility fosters creativity and innovation, helping firms to efficiently handle issues and satisfy changing market needs.

Improved Decision Making: Individuals who are adaptable are more likely to make successful judgments in unpredictable circumstances. Their capacity to assess events, weigh options, and make educated decisions helps them succeed in both personal and professional life.

Life is unpredictable, and not every situation comes with a set of instructions. Individuals who are adaptable can swiftly analyze a situation, examine various outcomes, and make decisions that are consistent with their aims and beliefs. Their adaptability allows people to modify their plans in response to new knowledge, resulting in improved outcomes and a sense of control in times of uncertainty.

Adaptation Strategies to Changing Circumstances:

1. Develop a development Mindset: View obstacles as opportunities for development and learning. Consider failures to be stepping stones toward success, and setbacks to be great lessons. The importance of mentality cannot be emphasized. Individuals with a growth mindset think that with dedication and hard effort, their talents and intelligence may be enhanced. They view failure as an opportunity to learn and develop rather than a reflection on their talents. This mindset enables people to approach

obstacles with a positive attitude and an openness to change.

2. Be Flexible: Adopt a flexible mindset and be prepared to explore new options. Avoid opposing change since it causes unneeded stress and impedes personal progress.
Change may be unsettling and might put our established habits and beliefs to the test. The more we fight change, however, the more difficult it is to adjust. Instead, keeping an open mind and being open to new ideas and possibilities can make the shift easier and less stressful.

3. Develop Emotional Intelligence: Emotional intelligence allows us to successfully understand and control our emotions, allowing us to adapt to change with grace and poise.
Recognizing and comprehending our own emotions, as well as the emotions of others, is part of emotional intelligence. When it comes to adapting to changing circumstances, self-awareness and empathy are essential. We

can respond to difficult events with clarity and balance if we are in tune with our emotions, helping us to make better decisions and preserve strong relationships during times of transition.

4. Create a Strong Support Network: Surround yourself with helpful and understanding people who can offer encouragement and direction through difficult times.
In times of transition, having a solid support network is critical. Having individuals who believe in us and our capacity to adapt, whether they be friends, family, mentors, or coworkers, may make a major impact in our path. They may provide vital insights, emotional support, and help us see things from other angles, allowing us to make better decisions at difficult circumstances.

5. Continuous Learning: Maintain your curiosity and seek knowledge on a regular basis. Lifelong learning provides us with the abilities we need to confidently adapt to new conditions.

The world is changing at a quick pace, and the only way to stay current is to keep learning. Accept the habit of lifelong learning, whether by formal schooling, reading, attending seminars, or seeking out new experiences. Continuous learning not only provides us with the skills required for change adaptation, but it also maintains our brains nimble and open to new possibilities.

The ability to adapt to changing circumstances allows us to negotiate the challenges of life with resilience and flexibility. Accepting change allows for personal development, innovation, and new possibilities. We may approach change with confidence and harness its potential for good development by cultivating a growth mindset, cultivating emotional intelligence, and remaining open to new experiences. Remember that life is an adaptation process, and those who accept change are better suited to flourish in it.

Finding the Right Balance for Success

Achieving great accomplishments in one's job, personal life, or both is frequently described as success. The pursuit of achievement, on the other hand, may be all-consuming, leaving people feeling overwhelmed and burned out. Long-term prosperity and total well-being require striking the correct balance between many facets of life. This article discusses the significance of finding the correct balance for success, the difficulties that individuals may experience, and ways for achieving harmony in various aspects of life.

Determining Success and Its Elements:

Success is a multidimensional idea that differs from one individual to the next. While accomplishing career milestones or financial prosperity is frequently included, it can also include personal fulfillment, meaningful connections, and a feeling of purpose. It is critical to define what success means to each individual and identify the important components that contribute to their well-being in order to establish the correct balance for success.

1. Professional Success: Achieving goals and milestones in one's job or business is a common definition of professional success. Promotions, recognition, financial growth, and job happiness are all examples of this.

2. Personal Fulfillment: A sense of pleasure and enjoyment generated from interests, passions, and personal growth is referred to as personal fulfillment. It entails finding delight in things other than employment and caring for one's physical, emotional, and mental well-being.

3. connections and Social Connections: Successful people build and maintain meaningful connections with family, friends, and coworkers. Support, contentment, and a sense of belonging are all provided by strong social ties.

4. Health and Well-Being: Without excellent health, success cannot be completely achieved.

Physical well-being, which includes exercise, right diet, and adequate relaxation, is essential for leading a healthy and successful life.

The Difficulties of Balancing Success:
Getting the perfect balance for success is a never-ending juggling act that can be impacted by a variety of challenges:

1. Time Constraints: Juggling several obligations might leave people with little time for personal interests and self-care.
2. Overcommitment: Saying yes to every opportunity or request might result in an overloaded calendar, making it difficult to prioritize efficiently.
3. FOMO: The fear of missing out on prospective chances or experiences can drive people to take on too much, leading to burnout.
4. The Prioritization Dilemma: Deciding which elements of life merit greater attention can be difficult since several areas may fight for attention.

5. Unrealistic Expectations: Having unrealistic expectations of oneself can lead to disappointment and a persistent feeling of inadequacy.

Balance-Achieving Techniques:

1. Establish Your Values and Priorities: Consider what is actually important to you and align your objectives and activities appropriately. Knowing your values and priorities can assist you in making decisions that will help you live a balanced and successful life.

2. Establish Boundaries: Learn to say no to obligations that do not line with your beliefs or that take up too much of your time. Setting limits helps you to focus on what is genuinely important while avoiding burnout.

3. Practice Time Management: Effective time management is essential for balancing numerous parts of life. Set priorities, make timetables, and make time for work, personal interests, and relationships.

Recognize that life is unpredictable, and being flexible helps you to adjust to changing situations without feeling overwhelmed.

4. Develop Self-Compassion: Be kind with yourself and recognize that it's normal to make errors or take breaks. Self-compassion assists you in maintaining a healthy perspective through difficult circumstances.

5. Learn to Delegate: When feasible, delegate work in both your professional and personal life. Recognize that you do not need to accomplish everything by yourself.

6. Mindfulness: Practice mindfulness to be present and completely engage in each moment, minimizing stress and anxiety over the past or future.

7. Assess and Adjust on a Regular Basis: Evaluate your life balance on a regular basis and make modifications as needed. Life is fluid, and what works for you one day may not work the next.

Professional Success and Balance:

1. Define Your Career Objectives and Make a strategy to attain Them: Define your career objectives and make a strategy to attain them. Having specific goals can help you stay focused and make decisions that are in line with your professional objectives.

2. Communicate with Your Boss: Communicate openly with your employer about your professional goals and any obstacles you may experience in managing work and family life.

3. Strive for Work-Life Integration: Rather of viewing work and personal life as distinct things, strive to blend them. When feasible, incorporate components of your personal life into your job routine and vice versa.

4. Prioritize chores: To prevent getting overwhelmed by a large to-do list, prioritize high-priority chores first.

Personal Fulfillment and Work:
1. Pursue Hobbies and Passions: Make time for hobbies that you truly like, such as painting, hiking, writing, or playing an instrument.

2. Invest in Learning: Seek out chances to learn and improve on a regular basis, whether through classes, workshops, or self-directed study.

3. Prioritize Self-Care Activities: To recharge and revitalize, prioritize self-care activities such as exercise, meditation, or spending time in nature.

Relationships and Social Connections Must Be Balanced:
1. Make Time for Quality connections: Whether it's a regular dinner date or a weekend vacation, make time for meaningful connections with family and friends.

2. Be Present in Relationships: Engage in active listening and real interest in the lives of those

you care about. Being present improves the quality of your interactions.

3. Encourage and encourage Each Other's ambitions: Encourage and encourage the ambitions and dreams of people around you. Personal and group achievement are enhanced by a supporting network.

Balancing Health and Happiness:
1. **Make Sleep a Priority:** Get adequate restful sleep to preserve your physical and emotional well-being.
2. **Include Exercise:** Exercise is important for general health and can enhance mood and energy levels.
3. **Consume Nutritious Foods:** To maintain energy and improve well-being, fuel your body with a well-balanced diet.

Finding the correct balance for success is a dynamic process that demands self-awareness, focus, and adaptability. You may establish a harmonious existence that leads to long-term success and general well-being by defining success on your own terms and understanding the value of personal fulfillment, relationships, and health. Accept flexibility, practice self-compassion, and check your life balance on a regular basis to ensure you are on track to reach your objectives and live a full and successful life. Remember that success is more than simply arriving at your objective; it is also about enjoying the road and finding joy in the process.

CONCLUSION

"The Destiny Blueprint" is a concept that explores the idea that each individual's life is guided by a predetermined plan or purpose, akin to a blueprint that outlines the path they are destined to follow. This concept has been a subject of contemplation and fascination for generations, as people seek to understand the underlying forces that shape their lives and the events that unfold.

Throughout history, various cultures and belief systems have embraced the notion of a destiny blueprint, often intertwined with ideas of fate, karma, or divine intervention. The belief in a higher power or universal design that governs our existence offers solace and meaning in the face of life's uncertainties and challenges. It encourages individuals to trust in a greater purpose and find comfort in the idea that everything happens for a reason.

However, the concept of the destiny blueprint is not without its skeptics. Critics argue that embracing such an idea may lead to passivity and a sense of helplessness, as individuals may feel constrained by a predetermined path. They advocate for a belief in free will, the power of individual choice, and the capacity to shape one's destiny through actions and decisions.

Finding a balance between the belief in destiny and the exercise of free will is a personal journey. For some, embracing the idea of a destiny blueprint provides a sense of guidance and faith in the grand tapestry of life. For others, it may be more empowering to believe in the potential for self-determination and the ability to forge their own path.

Regardless of individual beliefs, the concept of the destiny blueprint reminds us of the interconnectedness of all things and the intricate dance of cause and effect that shapes our lives. It prompts us to reflect on the significance of our actions and the ripples they create in the vast ocean of existence.

Ultimately, whether one believes in a predetermined destiny or the power of choice, the journey of life remains an adventure filled with twists and turns, triumphs and tribulations. Each of us navigates this journey with a unique combination of circumstances, experiences, and opportunities. Embracing the uncertainty of life with resilience, openness, and a willingness to learn allows us to grow and evolve, regardless of the role destiny may play.

The concept of the destiny blueprint is a captivating notion that sparks contemplation about the mysteries of life and the interplay of fate and free will. While the debate between destiny and free will continues, what remains clear is that every individual has the power to shape their character, actions, and response to the unfolding events. Finding meaning and purpose in life is an ever-evolving process, and each person's journey is a testament to the richness and complexity of the human experience.

www.ingramcontent.com/pod-product-compliance
Lightning Source LLC
Chambersburg PA
CBHW060951260726
48661CB00005B/1842